Can You See?

LEVEL 4

/igh/
/ar/

DECODABLES BY jump!

Teaching Tips

Blue Level 4

This book focuses on the phonemes **/igh/ar/**.

Before Reading

- Discuss the title. Ask readers what they think the book will be about. Have them briefly explain why.
- Ask readers to sort the words on page 3. Read the sounds and words together.

Read the Book

- Encourage readers to break down unfamiliar words into units of sound. Then, ask them to string the sounds together to create the words.
- Urge readers to point out when the focused phonics phonemes appear in the text.

After Reading

- Encourage children to reread the book independently or with a friend.
- Ask readers to name other words with /igh/ or /ar/ phonemes. On a separate sheet of paper, have them write the words out.

North American adaptations © 2024 Jump!
5357 Penn Avenue South
Minneapolis, MN 55419
www.jumplibrary.com

Decodables by Jump! are published by Jump! Library.

Library of Congress Cataloging-in-Publication Data is available at www.loc.gov or upon request from the publisher.

ISBN: 979-8-88996-816-0 (hardcover)
ISBN: 979-8-88996-817-7 (paperback)
ISBN: 979-8-88996-818-4 (ebook)

Photo Credits

Images are courtesy of Shutterstock.com. With thanks to Getty Images, Thinkstock Photo and iStockphoto. Cover – leungchopan. 4–5 – Dmytro Zinkevych, Svitlana Hulko. 6–7 – Inside Creative House, leungchopan. 8–9 – CandyBox Images, Africa Studio. 10–11 – Gatot Adri, JU.STOCKER. 12–13 – Ground Picture, Brylynskyi. 14–15 – rangizzz, Tewcaps. 16 – Shutterstock.

Can you sort all the words on this page into two groups?

Night

Charm

Words with **igh**

Might

Arm

Light

Barn

Right

Words with **ar**

Sight

Bar

Far

At the eye doctor, you can test your sight.

They will point a bright light at you.
It cannot harm you.

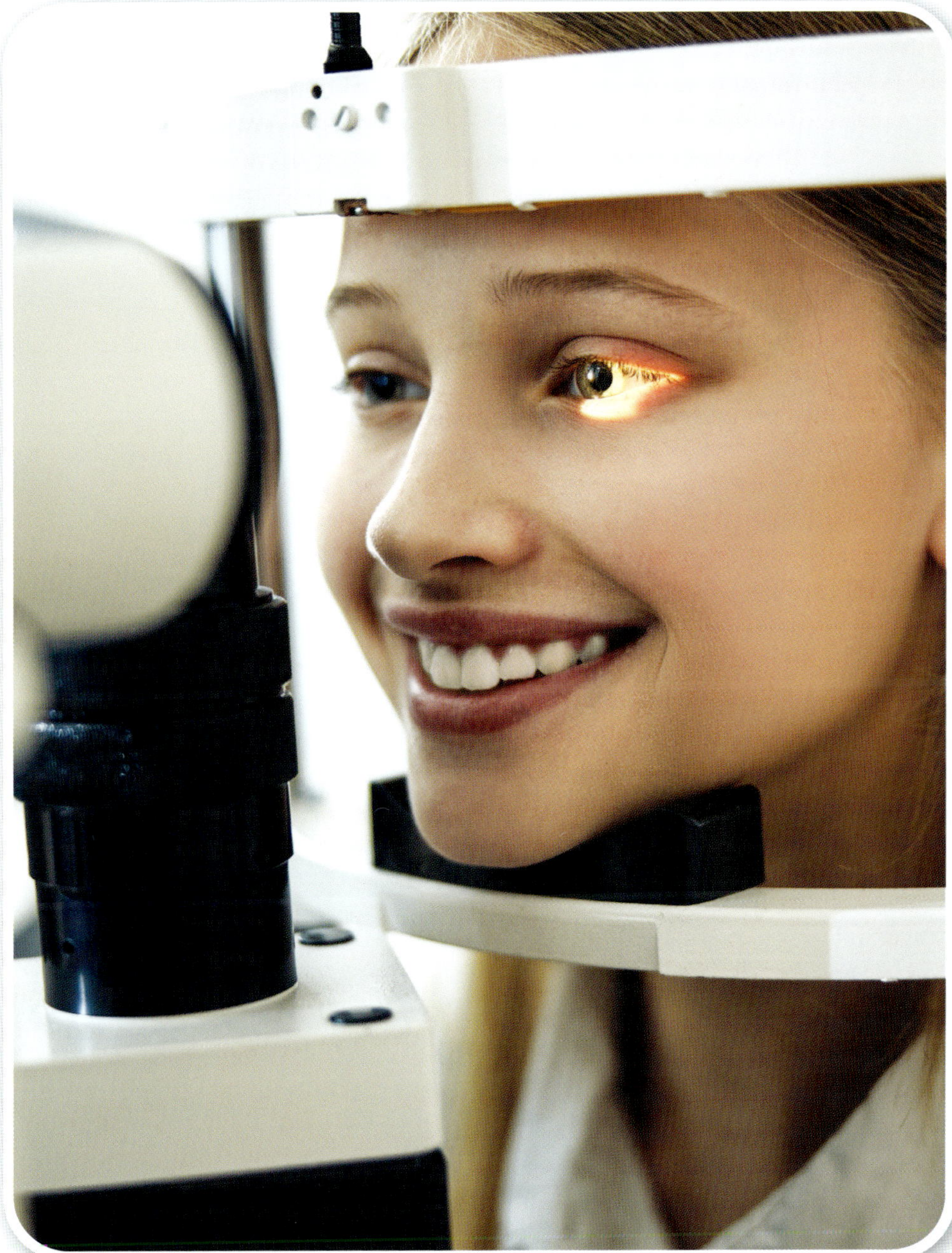

The chin rest will help you see the right spot.

They might have a chart for you to look at.

Can you see a big letter at the top?

Can you see the little letters?
Some might be hard to see.

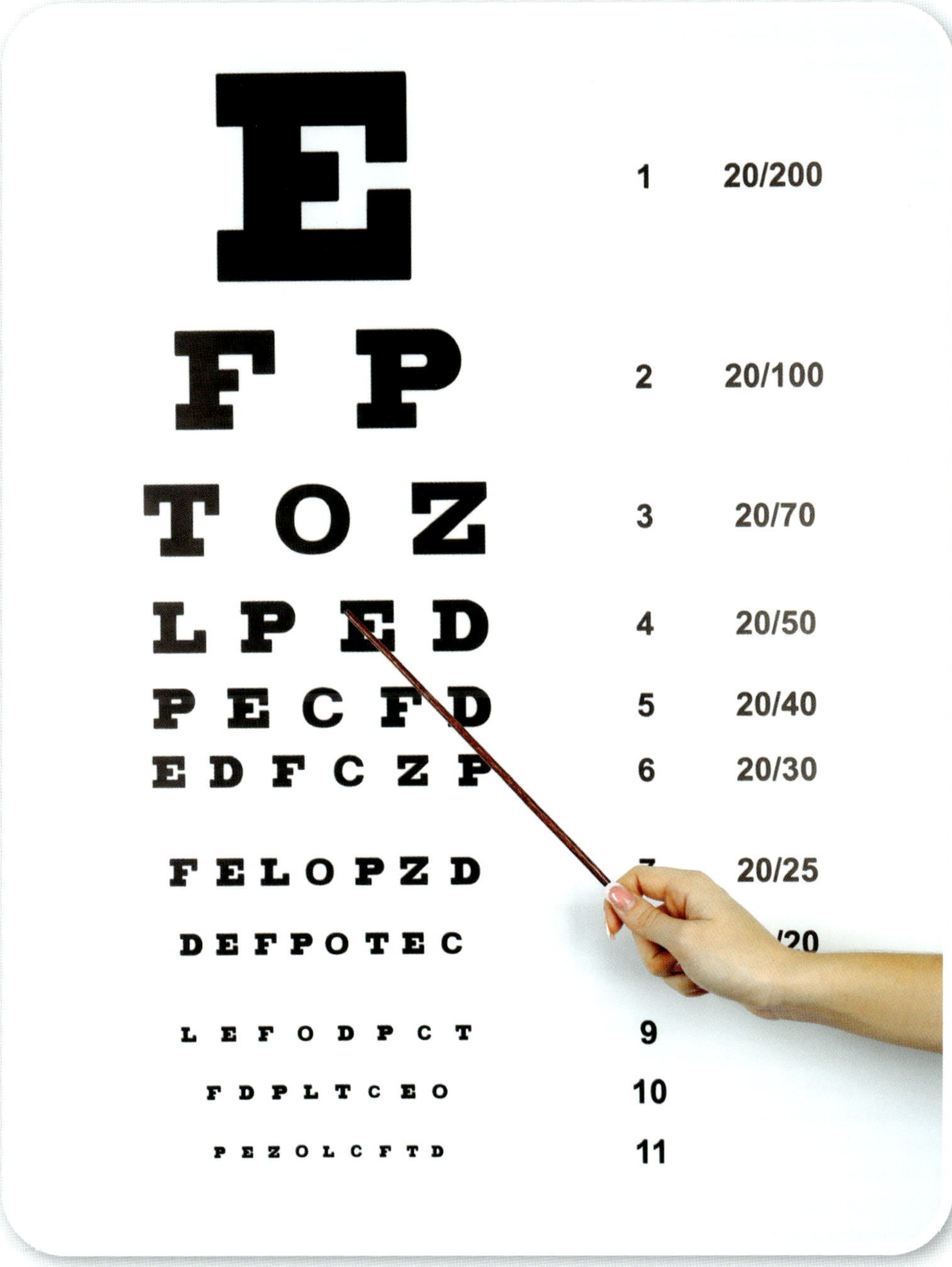

If you cannot see some letters,
you might need help to see better.

You might need to look at the letters with a lens.

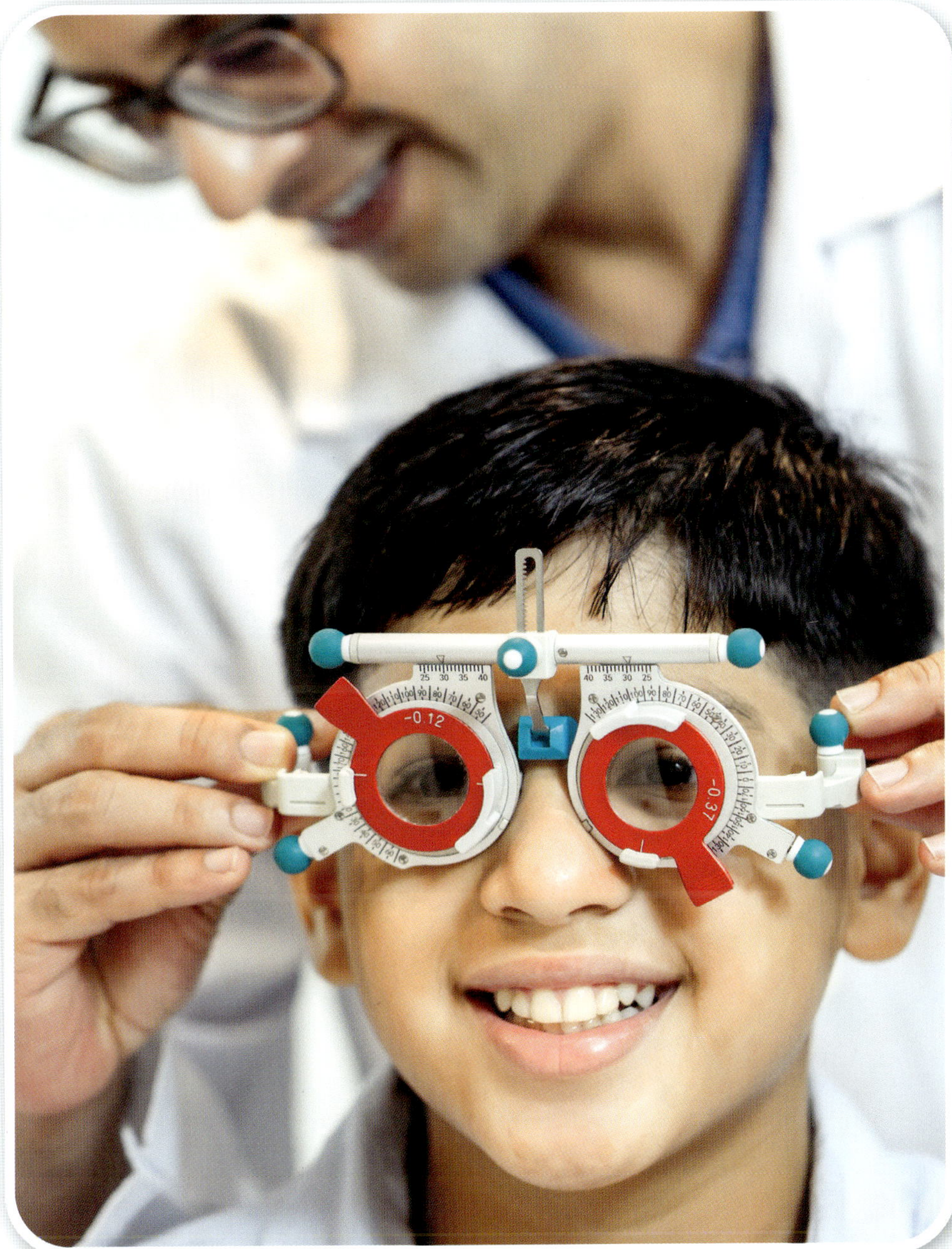

If you can see well with the lens, they might get you glasses.

This part is an arm. This part is the rim. This part is a lens.

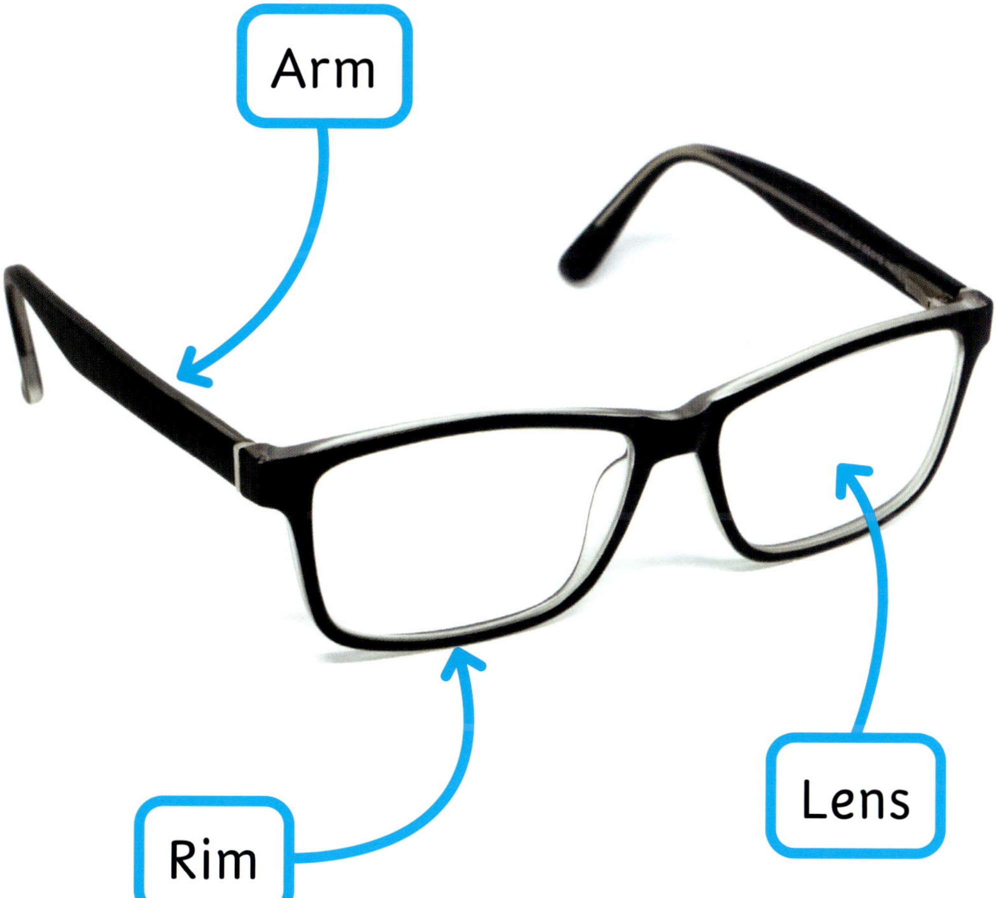

If you do need them, glasses will help you see better.

Glasses can help you better see things that are near and far.

Sound out each word. Does it have an /igh/ or /ar/ sound?

night

flight

jar

art